LOOSED II

Stories in Rhyme

By Larry Davis

Loosed II
Copyright © 2017 by Larry Davis

ISBN: 978-1546568780

Contents

Preface

LOOSED II, *Stories in Rhyme*, has been a long time coming. The first story in rhyme was written in the late eighty's. When I wrote the first one I had no clue of the impact that they would have on people.

I'm eternally grateful for this God-given ability to express the thoughts and emotions of people from every walk of life, past, present, and future.

I believe that many of these poems are the untold stories of strangers, speaking and sharing their story. Some of the poems are biblically inspired, but give depth that could have only come from God.

A Special thanks to my wife Helen for all her support and love over the span of our 46-year marriage. To my children Angela, Mary, and Timothy. As well as my grandchildren Amia, Cienna, Malia, and Timothy Jr.

Additionally, special thanks to Caroline Meyers, my spiritual daughter and the inspiration for the first poem in the first Loosed. Caroline, your sincere critics have been invaluable and are appreciated. You could not have been more passionate about them if you wrote them yourself. To Kelly Madison for listening with an open heart in all sincerity. The tears you shed in response to hearing each poem did not go unnoticed. To Mr. Alvin Davis, for inspiring me to take the next step and share these with the world. Your encouraging words were priceless. To Mara D. Johnson for her dedication to this project and tireless efforts to transition it from dream to reality. As well as a whole host of people over the years that encouraged me.

It is my sincere hope and desire that you enjoy taking a glimpse into people's greatest disappointments, their love, their hate, their moments of clarity.

Mama

My life is ending
I'm deathly sick,
the doctors have told me
I won't go quick.

A terrible illness
which has no cure
death would be slow,
but also sure.

I want my mama
the food she cooks.
I'll put on weight
and get back my looks.

"Mama please help me
come see your son!"
But Mama can't hear me
her life is now done.

She never stopped loving me
I didn't know why
I was good for nothing,
but to make Mama cry.

A washed-up hustler
a zero at best.
With a heart full of evil
lodged in my chest.

My daddy had left us
we went it alone.
Mama clothed and fed me
until I was grown.

She had taught me Jesus
at an early age,
but I was rebellious
and filled with rage.

It seemed we had nothing
and what had God done
and that Jewish Carpenter
they say is His Son.

The Bible was nothing
a tool of the man
to keep us as pawns
in the games that he ran.

I wanted to hustle
get down in the streets.
I meant to get over
to land on my feet.

Get some fast women
build me a stash
drive a long ride
and rake in the cash.

I hit the streets early
Mama's preaching I fled
entered the game running
determined to get ahead.

But the streets are a game
not easily played
its constant changes
left my nerves frayed.

To meet it's challenges
and constant stress.
Drained me mentally
and robbed me of rest.

This constant pressure
which just won't stop,
only the strongest of men
can stay on top.

Those fast city streets
had proven too much
my legs of pride broken
I reached for a crutch.

I began to smoke crack
most evil addiction,
which shattered my life
with bondage and affliction.

I called upon Scottie
and he beamed me there,
an out of body experience
that took me somewhere.

Flooded my being
with pleasure unknown,
the purest of ecstasy
that made my soul groan.

I was instantly hooked
that very first hit.
Nothing I'd experienced
had prepared me for it.

He took me to that place
the holy land of crack
and I've spent twenty years
trying to go back.

I'd leave home on missions
chasing rocks to burn
sometimes for months
before I'd return.

Small time dealers
waiting for licks
and burned out rock stars
busy turning tricks.

Abandoned children
and crack babies too.
The world of crack fiends
mostly hidden from view.

Mama would talk to me,
but I just wouldn't hear.
My trip back to crack land
seemed always so near.

Just one more time
let me take that flight.
I pleaded with Scottie
both day and night.

"It's in the next hit
keep trying you'll see,
if you don't give up
I'll beam you to me."

I'd hit and I'd hit
and I' hit it again.
My mind playing tricks
as paranoia sets in.

"Mr. windows," as always
is standing outside
you run from your peep hole
to somewhere to hide.

Coke bugs are every where
I'm climbing the walls
strange voices whispering
just down the hall.

Other people are with me
who do what I do,
they also are tripping
and paranoid too.

I'd really been had
Scottie made me a fool.
One trip to his holy land
had given him rule.

He took from me all
that's important in life
I never had a home
no children or wife.

When I finally got word
that Mama had died.
I fell to my knees
and sorrowfully cried.

Who would even care
now Mama was gone
as the oil of despair
penetrated my bones.

I entered the rehabs
did outpatient too,
but that monster yet ruled
when all was through.

I finally gave up
and ceased even trying.
Destroyed by crack rocks
and now told that I'm dying.

I was so angry
that nothing could be done,
Mama's prayers had failed
to save her dear son.

I decided to end it
why drag it out,
"God failed you Mama!"
At her picture I shout.

Where was this God
that she loved so much,
religion was a game
just a poor man's crutch.

I looked in the mirror
and recoiled at the sight,
then took out my pistol
to end it that night.

I cried "God if you're real
then give me a sign!"
Crack has destroyed
this poor life of mine.

I'm no longer a man,
but mere skin and bone.
I'm tired of suffering
and being alone.

God if you're real
if you show me somehow.
Just like my mama
before you I'll bow.

Then on the radio
next door that night,
a preacher was preaching
and I saw the light.

I saw Jesus loved me
and really did care
as I knelt in the toilet
and accepted Him there.

Never such peace
I'd felt in my life,
as the moment I received
the Lord Jesus Christ.

Jesus has healed me
and destroyed Satan's hold.
I preach for Him now
and have joy in my soul.

God gave me a wife
she's really good looking,
and just like my mama
that woman be cooking.

I've regained my health
and my life is on track.
All that crack stole
my Savior gave back.

Scottie would never
have beamed me again,
but my high in Jesus
will never have end.

He too has beamed me
and took me somewhere
and one day forever
I'll be with Him there.

The Lord Jesus has saved me
and made me free,
yes the God of my mama
has answered her plea.

Rahway

I cannot focus
this can't be real,
I'm looking down
at the man I've killed.

His feet are dressed
in brand new shoes.
The last I guess
he'll ever use.

I've panicked now
and want to run.
I said, "Oh Lord,
what have I done?"

A life of its own
this temper of mine,
I've messed things up
real bad this time.

I'd heard Mama sobbing
earlier tonight,
begging God to save me
to show me the light.

That really riled me
couldn't they see?
I was alright
if they'd let me be.

Cursing and screaming
I break for the door,
my daddy restraining me
Mama prone on the floor.

"Let me go Dad!"
I scream and yell
"If God is so good
why send folks to hell?"

"Just let me go Dad!"
I tell him again
"Why all the good stuff
have to be sin?"

I stormed out the door
and jumped in my car.
Then squealed across town
to the, "Open Door Bar."

I carry my "piece"
just in case,
some dude gets nasty
and jumps in my face.

Mom and Dad praying
was all I could think,
as I sat on a stool
and swallowed my drink.

I went to the john
to "toke" a few hits,
my rage so demonic
I'm now throwing fits.

I returned to the bar
to find some fool,
has found the nerve
to sit on my stool.

With unbridled rage
I threw him from the seat,
after blasting away
he died at my feet.

I stood there grieving
in that noisy dive,
while waiting tensely
for police to arrive.

Did he go to heaven?
Would he be alright?
These questions swirling
in my head that night.

Policemen stream in
my legs now fail,
in my heart I know
he's gone to hell.

To say I'm sorry
is more than fact.
I've taken in anger
what I can't give back.

All my young life
I've been a hot head,
and now in this barroom
a man is shot dead.

My daddy a preacher
my mother saved too.
Both lived the life
so I knew what to do.

I had been loved,
their youngest son.
My older brother Ray
loved God a ton.

But I was my own man
I knew how to fight,
and preached the gospel
of my left and right.

I thought I was hard
and knew what was best,
and now I had blasted
this man in his chest.

The police draw guns
and give the command.
I lay down my weapon
and put up my hands.

Placed under arrest
they read me my rights,
then turned me around
and cuffed me real tight.

This is so messed up
I've killed this man.
My circulation cut off
by the cuffs on my hands.

Down at the station
I'm allowed one call.
I talked to my mother
who says nothing at all.

The news that I gave her
her good life destroys,
I've taken from two moms
their dearly beloved boys.

Mom finally exhales
and screams a loud cry.
A sound of such anguish
I wanted to die.

Knowing this tragedy
had caused such pain,
I wished from my heart
I'd died with the slain.

I said to her "Momma
I'll be alright,"
but knew I was lying
to us both that night.

I thought of the slain
and his mother too,
when she gets the news
what will she do?

I wanted to stop thinking
of how she would feel,
the pain and suffering
for her son I'd killed.

Did he have a father,
an older brother too?
When they see me in court
what will they do?

They posted my bail
and the very next day,
my Mom and Dad met me
with my older brother Ray.

Not wanting to face them
I felt so ashamed.
What could I tell them
after ruining our name?

I could see the headlines
tomorrow's news feature,
"Local man slain
by the son of a preacher!"

My Dad and Mom both
wear deep worry lines.
Their son is a murderer
and facing hard time.

My mom looks frail
I can't stand the sight.
It seemed she'd aged
many years overnight.

All the way home
we rode with the dead,
our unseen passenger
and no words were said.

His life is now gone
and I'm to blame.
I know in my heart,
I won't be the same.

My soul weighed down
with my burden of sin.
I'm alone in my room,
with the walls caving in.

My mother and father
asleep in their room.
It's always been peaceful,
but now filled with gloom.

I awaken my father
and fall to my knees.
I ask him to help me
to pray with me please.

Mom and Dad hugged me
and calling for Ray,
we all knelt together
and began to pray.

I said, "Lord I'm sorry
I've made such a mess,
I've killed a poor man
with a shot to the chest."

"I've let Satan use me
to cause so much pain,
I've killed this poor man
and I'm going insane"

"I deserve to be punished
and know I'll do time,
but I ask you to save
this poor soul of mine."

That's when it happened,
Jesus entered my heart.
And because of his mercy
I have a new start.

Twenty-five to life
in Rahway State Pen,
I'm sentenced to serve
with the angriest of men.

But here I have peace,
though Rahway is hell.
I have his assurance
that things will be well.

I talk of Christ Jesus
to all who will hear.
The Lord is my comfort
and keeps me from fear.

Ray and my parents
often I see,
they visit this prisoner
God's Son has made free.

Queen

My life back home
was one living hell.
Daddy beat Momma
and raped me as well.

I finally left home
in my late teens,
hit the streets running
became known as "Queen."

The streets were mean
definitely didn't play,
no one had sympathy
for a teen runaway.

If I was going to make it
I was on my own,
with my few clothes
and a cheap cell phone.

Soaked up the streets
and learned one thing,
It's what you take
not what you bring.

I learned how to hustle
elevated my play.
There's no free ride
at the end of the day.

Learning to be hard
not showing how I felt,
playing the hand
that I had been dealt.

South side of Chicago
you hustle every cent,
for groceries and light bill
and paying the rent.

You can't expect anything,
But take what you need.
From what Queen wore,
to smoking her weed.

Like this lame
who just got to town.
I gave him the eye
til he was hot to get down.

This guy was flirting
with every girl in sight.
Spending long green
and on my radar that night.

I walked right over,
said I was "Queen."
Eyeing the biggest bank roll,
that I'd ever seen.

I'd make a quick work
and trim this lame.
He'd be no match,
for me and my game.

I have flavor
that men love to view,
high yellow color
and wavy hair too.

Men get a look
at the way that I'm stacked
they see why I'm called Queen
and stop in their tracks.

I knew he was hooked
I could see it in his eyes.
He was already convinced,
he had Queen as his prize.

I wasn't amused
at the things he said.
The man was confident
He'd be sharing my bed.

I had to hurry
Speed up my game,
before I get nasty
and hurt this lame.

Like I'm some weak sister
From way down south,
he don't bring it in check
I'll bust a cap in his mouth.

I went to the room
where the trick stayed,
ripped him off easily
and did a quick fade.

It would be morning
before he knew,
I had fleeced his pockets
and took his car too.

But I had grown weary
of playing games,
Cons and hustlers
Tricks and Lames.

There had to be better
somewhere for me,
I wanted something different
and longed to be free.

I then met a man
who spake about sin,
saying Jesus would save me
If I just let Him in.

I took a long look
wondering what's his game,
he certainly didn't look
like any other lame.

The man kept talking
I finally saw light,
and received Jesus Christ
as savior that night.

My constant companion
who loves his "Queen"
who finally met Jesus
and made Him her "King."

You too can be saved
and washed from sin,
if you open your heart
and let Jesus in.

A New Beginning

The year 1939
the darkest of hour,
Hitler and the Nazis
had come to power.

Hitler blamed the Jew
for Germany's strife.
His message touching people
from all walks of life.

A mesmerizing speaker
The masses were fooled,
and made this man Chancellor
giving him rule.

They were the master race,
so plain to see.
To this Aryan myth
they all agree.

The time soon arose
his power absolute.
The masses make him leader,
"Heil Hitler," they salute.

The Fuhrer of Germany
and their Lord supreme,
the masses are ecstatic
and shout and scream.

He had a master plan,
he knew what to do.
Ridding planet earth
of the dirty little Jew.

I was a Jew,
recently from France.
I played violin
and studied dance.

I too heard the rot
that Hitler put out.
Just a flash in the pan
we had little doubt.

The civilized world
would never stand by,
and let this man break
The treaty of Versailles.

I was really surprised
they'd let him this far,
hadn't these same people
plunged the world into war?

I thought of my family,
back home in Berlin.
Things must be terrible
with the Reich closing in.

I thought about Mama
and dear Papa too,
there never existed
a much prouder Jew.

My older sister Deborah
and little Mary Anne.
My older brother Adam
to be destroyed by this man.

We bore the weight
of this man's wrath.
He unleashed a war
destroying all in its path.

Seeing the clouds gathering
I knew I must flee,
boarded a ship to America
the land of the free.

We climbed aboard
the cruise ship St. Louis.
Nine hundred souls,
both Jew and Jewess.

Steaming across the waters
of the icy Atlantic.
Fleeing our home,
both desperate and frantic.

At last New York Harbor
a most beautiful sight,
but Franklin D. Roosevelt
extinguished that light.

Unable to believe
we all gasp for breath.
He's sending us back
to the Nazi death.

Seeing Queen Liberty
fade into the mist.
How could Roosevelt
betray us like this?

As we're heading home
to the land of our birth.
There was no one to help us
in all the earth.

Taken captive by Nazis
the same ones we'd fled.
Within a short time,
would we all be dead?

What would become of us?
We pondered in our heart,
being loaded on trains,
as our long journey starts.

We're fed once a day,
little water to drink.
The cars jammed packed
and starting to stink.

Its sweltering hot,
in the summertime heat.
We all were sweating,
shoes wet on our feet.

At the Warsaw Ghetto
we finally arrive.
Whose people are starved
and barely alive.

I never could have imagined,
a place of such horror.
Such filth and decay
and unending sorrow.

The vermin and lice
did everywhere abound.
We're packed so tight
we can barely turn around.

It hung so heavy
a death wish mood.
Everyone engrossed
with where to find food.

Disease and sickness
had taken their toll.
Just sticks and bones
we all look old.

They came and got me
and took me away,
with quite a few others
that eventful day.

To a wooded area
we all were led
and were told to lay down
on top of the dead.

The soldiers proceeded
to shoot us too.
Systematic elimination
of the unwanted Jew.

The soldiers were joyful
and having much fun.
Then one grabbed me
and told me to run.

I heard them laughing
aiming rifles at me,
I headed for the woods
and hid in a tree.

They finally gave up,
after I wasn't found.
At last I accepted,
that no one's around.

Then asked The Lord God
if He's really there?
Didn't He see?
Did He even care?

Where was the Messiah
He promised to send?
Now was the time
to deal with these men.

I was surprised
to hear Him speak,
the God of my fathers
as my knees went weak.

"I've already come,
to die for the lost.
Two thousand years ago
I hung on the cross."

That had to be Jesus
It couldn't be true.
Jesus is the Savior
of both Gentile and Jew?

I fell to my knees
confessing my sin,
and asked Him to save me
and really come in.

He came in and saved me
for real that day,
so glad I had questioned
and started to pray.

The fighting soon over,
the war finally ended.
That mad man was stopped
from what he intended.

I finally united
with Ma and Pa too.
Adam and my sisters
God saved the Jews.

I found a little church
at last baptized.
Behind those little walls
the real truth lies.

My family came to Jesus
and loves Him too.
Old things are gone
we're all brand new.

Walter Ray

I had no peace,
my mind wrapped tight.
I wanted to end it
to go out with a fight.

My future now hopeless
I long for the grave.
She treated me like trash
after all that I gave.

My wife had left me
a few years back,
ran off with some low life
who hooked her on crack.

I worked for the city
for twenty long years
and now with a furlough
they end my career.

But I won't go quietly
like some trick lame,
I'll get me some payback
and make me a name.

My mind was made up
as I walked out the door,
I'd take a few with me
and even the score.

I then went shopping
and bought me a gun,
an AR-15
to get the job done.

Learned in the military
had been a crack shot
and still had my touch
so things would get hot.

Up on a hill
I was planning to go
and take out the drivers
on the freeway below.

On Washington Bridge
I'd bottle them in,
trap them like cattle
and let the slaughter begin.

I could see the panic
of husband and wife,
as I zeroed in
and began to take life.

Cars spinning out
as I let bullets fly,
as one by one
their occupants die.

Trapped on the freeway
with no place to go,
some jump from the bridge
into the waters below.

Some freeze in their seats
like a scene from Star Wars,
as bullets hit gas tanks
and blow up their cars.

In a blaze of glory
I'm leaving this life,
avenged for my job,
my home and my wife.

Linda and that dude
will see one day,
the movie that's made
about me Walter Ray.

I've settled the score
at last been avenged,
my name has been glorified
and the city unhinged.

My plan now solidified
I turn on the TV,
the face of a preacher
there speaking to me.

He spoke of forgiveness
and letting things go.
As if aware of my plan
but how did he know?

And why should I care?
Preachers were wimps,
half of them robbers
and the other half pimps.

And what had God done,
to save my job?
I meant to go through
with killing some slobs!

He could have stopped Linda
from leaving me too,
but Big Daddy God
what did He do?

I'll get some justice.
I'll make someone pay.
Don't dare preach to me
these chumps better pray!

The very next morning
just as I planned,
I gathered my weapon
and over them stand.

Raising my rifle
my targets in sight,
I then pull the trigger,
but the bullet flies right.

What had just happened?
How had I missed?
I chose another target
after shaking my fist.

I pointed my rifle
and took careful aim,
then squeezed the trigger
but more of the same.

I then heard His voice
**"Walter Ray it's not right,
I Jesus of Nazareth
will show you the light."**

**"It's totally wrong Ray
what you're trying to do,
these people are innocent
and done nothing to you!"**

I fell on my face
and tearfully repent,
crying out to Jesus
till totally spent.

I lay down that night
with peace in my heart,
knowing I was given
a brand-new start.

In a Spirit filled church
the very next day,
I knelt at an altar
with a Preacher to pray.

I told the Lord Jesus,
I wanted to be free
and I'd serve Him for life
if he would save me.

That very moment
He gave me His life
and later restored
my marriage and wife.

The Lord had saved Linda
now delivered from crack
and it gave me delight
to see her come back.

Where I had been angry
now peace in my life,
found only in Jesus
my pearl of great price.

Another O.D.

I see another junkie
walking real fast,
nodding my way
as he's going past.

I'm aching and shaking
from my feet to my head.
My body craves heroin
and has to be fed.

This heroin jones
is some kind of mean,
I'm totally strung out
a junky dope fiend.

My need seems greater
with each passing day,
junk is my master
and master don't play.

My nerves are frayed
and I can't be still.
If I have to get violent
best believe that I will.

It's nothing nice
the things that I do.
I'll smile in your face
and steal from you.

I have to pay up
if I want to nod,
scouring the streets
feeling cursed by God.

And what has God done
to help me break free,
the rehabs and programs
do nothing for me.

If God is so great
why don't He step in.
Instead of letting me
slide deeper in sin.

If he really heard me
those times I prayed,
why has my death
been so long delayed.

Why won't He hear
my heart's daily plea,
that he would grant me
one final O.D.

Another O.D.
that's all I need
one lethal hot hit
and I will be freed.

Just wishful thinking
as I head for the park
and hide in the shadows
to await my mark.

I see her coming
as I kneel in the bush
then jump from the shadows
and give her a push.

Grabbing her purse
after knocking her down,
what was she expecting
in this part of town.

I rifle her purse
my shakes have gone bad,
her constant screaming
is making me mad.

"Woman I won't hurt you,
but you best shut down!
I can't have some hero
coming around"

A fat roll of bills
just what I need,
I head for my dealer
with all due speed.

But my dealer is missing
nowhere to be found,
at the end of my rope
I fall to the ground.

I cry out to God
with all of my might,
people recoiling
from my smell that night.

Can't God see
that I have to cop?
This pain is unbearable
and just won't stop.

My shakes intensify
and just won't quit,
I'm now in the midst
of a withdrawal fit.

Then I saw it
as plain as could be,
God wouldn't answer
a junkie like me.

I got to my feet
and staggered away
and vowed in my heart
to never again pray.

I couldn't score anywhere
not a dealer in sight,
as I staggered back
to the park that night.

There a lone voice,
long after dark.
Preaching good news
there in the park.

He talked about Jesus
coming to make us all free,
even burned out dope fiends
and junkies like me.

He spoke of his love
and his power to save.
How Jesus could deliver me
from my wrong doing ways.

His message like water
to a dry thirsty land,
as I clung to each word
that came from the man.

There in that instant
God answering my prayer.
He had been listening
and really did care.

I walked to the man
and fell at his feet.
He then stopped preaching
and smiled real sweet.

I saw such love
and compassion for me.
The man inside the junkie
I knew he could see.

He fell to his knees
and hugged me real tight,
saying call on Jesus
with all of my might.

That gospel message
that never grows old,
again worked wonders
and saved my soul.

Yes Jesus saved me
and made me brand new.
He's now my Master.
with heroin I'm through.

Yes grateful to God
I shall forever be.
I'm hooked on Jesus
and can't O.D!

The Champ

I was born in Chicago
on a cold winters night
I grew up with nothing
But a talent to fight.

I was young and cocky
and knew I was good.
And took all challenges
where I lived in the hood.

Chicago's southside
was my stomping ground,
but even beyond there
word was getting around.

They called me "The Breezer"
I was one cool poppa,
a one punch danger
a real show stopper.

A Pro-trainer saw me
called "Southside Slim"
and asked me to come out
and train at his gym.

This was my chance
I showed up the next night.
And was tutored by Slim,
in the sweet science of fight.

The day finally came,
my first fight as a pro.
In the very first round
a stunning KO.

I knocked out opponents
in rapid succession.
I set my sights on the title
and trained to perfection.

I stood the boxing world
upon its ears.
As I battered opponents,
and reduced them to tears.

Most of my opponents
were helped out the ring.
The experts knew,
I was destined to be king.

Every man that I fought
I went for his head,
my opponents now faced me
with terror and dread.

I challenged the Champion
to a world title fight,
but that aging imposter
was shaking with fright.

He feared what I would do
if he climbed in the ring.
I'd take his title
and become the new King.

His fights were a joke
the Champ on the run,
when everyone knew
that I was number one.

The day finally came
my goal in sight,
I signed with the Champ
for a showdown fight.

Six million dollars
my share of the purse,
I'd take his title
or leave in a hearse.

The night of the fight
the stadium was packed,
Pay-per-view odds
put the Champion on his back.

The bell finally sounded,
the house on its feet.
As I went for his head,
like a tiger for meat.

I banged him on top
and then dancing back,
three blows to the body
and heard something crack.

I could see him wincing
and pain on his face,
I again moved in
and quickened the pace.

The Champ covered up
and refused to go down.
As the bell finally sounded
to end the first round.

I went to my corner
and consulted with Slim,
said I was on track
and would soon finish him.

We entered round two
I made a full charge,
the Champ began withering
under a two-handed barrage.

I pounded his body,
remembering the crack.
The Champ was in pain,
but vainly fought back.

I threw more blows,
to his body and head.
Expecting him to fall,
like a sack full of lead.

But the man kept fighting
and earned my respect,
I had expected in round two
to lay him on deck.

The bell then sounded
we went to our seats.
I glanced the Champs way
and saw a man in defeat.

The next bell sounded
we came out for round three,
I landed a swift uppercut
and buckled his knees.

I saw the Champ stagger
and clutch his chest,
I then threw the blow
that sent him to rest.

The ref counted ten
and ended the fight.
I became the Heavyweight Champ
of the World that night.

I was ecstatic
and ran around the ring.
The Breezer was bad
the boxing worlds King.

The Heavyweight belt
I hugged to my chest,
of all the world's fighters,
I was number one best.

But over in the corner
The Champ was still out,
as the doc worked over him
long after the bout.

I waited in my locker
with a cold sense of dread.
Until getting the news
the Champ was now dead.

How could this happen?
This was my night.
No way to rejoice,
at the outcome of the fight.

My joy and jubilation
had now turned to pain.
Filled with such anguish
I feared going insane.

A Man was now dead
behind some stupid fight.
I wished with my heart
to make everything right.

Slim tried to comfort me,
These things happen he said.
But all I could think of
was this man lying dead.

I had seen the champ
clutching his chest,
and went charging in
to lay him to rest.

What had I proved?
That I had the best hands?
And now I'm responsible,
for killing this man.

I hung up my gloves
in the locker that night,
I had no more intention
to ever again fight.

I then faced the press
with tears in my eyes,
and the poor man's family
to apologize.

I left Slim's gym
with the fight world done.
I didn't want to party
or indulge with fun.

I gave away money
trying to buy peace.
But nothing I did
would bring me release.

I finally sunk down
into deep depression,
no longer caring
about self or possessions.

I ended up broke
and out on the streets.
Begging for handouts
and something to eat.

I had let myself become
a pitiful sight.
But I just couldn't shake,
what happened that night.

I then became addicted
to doing Crystal Meth.
Desiring in my heart
to join Champ in death.

But God was merciful
to me one night,
He picked me up
and put me back in the fight.

A young man walked up
with his Bible in hand.
He knew who I was
saying Christ understands.

He told me of rest
in Jesus I'd find.
That only His blood
would give peace of mind.

The fight wasn't over
I still could win.
I'd find in Christ mercy
and forgiveness of sin.

I gave him my hand
to lead me to Christ.
Who gave me real peace
for the first time in my life.

I now preach for Jesus
and back in life's ring.
He's the true Champion
and the number one King.

Nothing Said

I'm so exhausted
and want to leave,
but sit and wait
and quietly grieve.

I know he'll soon
be coming in.
And I'll have to face
his wrath again.

Another weekend
he's gone AWOL,
he didn't come home
or even call.

He staggers in
comes to our bed,
I lay there trembling
with covered head.

I take a peep
and see he's mad,
wrinkled clothes
and smelling bad.

I know he's broke
without one cent,
has blown the bills
and all the rent.

Same old pattern
I often see,
he comes home broke
and jumps on me.

He snatches the cover
from off my head,
his eyes are squinted
and bloodshot red.

The man's a beast
when he gets like this,
he makes a growl
and cocks his fist.

"Baby don't!!"
I softly plead,
then move away
with lighting speed.

"Woman," he shouts,
"What's wrong with you!"
Suddenly he's beating me
with his shoe.

I covered my head
and crawled away.
"Don't mess with me!"
I hear him say.

His rage and terror
in middle of the night,
his face is twisted
and demonic in sight.

He follows me
now breathing hard.
As I flee in terror,
into the back yard.

I wanted to scream,
but did not dare.
No way I'd live
till help got there.

I beg him softly,
"Baby please!"
And kneel before him
on my knees.

His intent to hurt me
was crystal clear,
I arise and run
in total fear.

He cuts me off
and knocks me down.
But I'm still afraid
to make much sound.

Again he's beating me
with his shoe
and stomps me in
my stomach too.

He finally ceases,
his rage now spent.
Then swaggers off
like the proper gent.

Later that night
he crawls in bed,
I feel so used
and nothings said.

Then at last
he falls asleep.
Out of bed
I silently creep.

Seven long years
I've been abused,
violently beaten
and sexually misused.

I've had enough
he's sealed his doom,
with hate filled purpose
I leave the room.

I grab a knife
and return again,
then raise my hands
to plunge it in.

His deeds will end
and cease for good.
His eyes then opened
and understood.

He sees the blade
now heading his way,
then makes a sound
and rolls away.

I saw him tripping
down the stairs
as he fled the house
in his under wear.

I then fell down
upon my knees.
and said "Lord Jesus
help me please!"

Then His voice spoke
loud and clear,
"Yes call on me
for I Am near."

That night Lord Jesus
saved my soul,
gave me peace
and made me whole.

I live for Jesus
and finally see,
my husband completely
change toward me.

He came to Jesus
and loves Him too.
Our wretched marriage
He made brand new.

He gets my coat
and opens doors,
takes me shopping
in finest stores.

He lavishes me
with God's love too
and sticks to me
like crazy glue.

Some nights he sits
beside our bed
and holds my hand
and nothing's said.

My Lady

My father a Preacher
and prayed all night.
I knew the truth,
but wouldn't do right.

My name is Wallace
from the West Texas hills,
but moved to Chicago
and hoped to find thrills.

But found the wrong crowd
introduced me to crack
and a terrible monkey
is now riding my back.

I was beamed by Scottie
who took me some place,
the smell and fragrance
and smoke in my face.

Often arrested
no money for bail.
I'd then talk to God
as I sat in my cell.

I'd pray real hard
down on my knees.
Beg God to help me,
to let me out please.

If He would just help me
I'd leave the drug scene,
find me some treatment
and get myself clean.

He'd always answer
my tears He'd wipe,
but moment I'm free
go back to the pipe.

I'd try hard to kick
but always gave in,
that monster crack
would always win.

That demon be calling
and just won't quit.
Telling myself
I'll stop at one hit.

That voice then whispers
"What can that hurt?"
Knowing that I've folded
falling back into the dirt.

Some of you know
understand how it feels,
you try to resist him
but your "inner man" yields.

You feel so at home
that moment so ripe,
pull out your lighter
and drag on the pipe.

You draw in the smoke
it dances so sweet,
that warm fiery rush
from head to feet.

What should I call her,
who consumes my life?
I call her my sweetheart,
my baby, my wife.

I must leave her altar
my resources gone,
she knows I'll return
I can't leave her alone.

She looks up and smiles
my cravings she's fed.
I long to return
and join her in bed.

Reading my thoughts
she knows I won't quit.
Till I score enough money
to return for more hits.

I look over my shoulder
the woman I see,
arms still outstretched
still calling to me.

I feel so defeated
after answering her call.
God alone knows
the shame of it all.

How had it happened
fell so far down,
where is that young man
I brought to this town?

I thought of my father
and his all-night prayer,
our little frame house
and longed to be there.

I felt such despair
and wanted to be free,
to be rid of the woman
and her voice calling me.

The God of my father
suddenly spoke clear,
drowned out the woman
that spoke in my ear.

"Time has come Wallace
you can be free!
From world's foundation
you've belonged to me."

My time in the city
had broken my health,
now leaving Chicago
with no earthly wealth.

I jumped on a freight train
with only a comb,
as cold empty boxcars
carried me home.

Knocked on the door
my father was there,
he warmly embraced me
as we knelt in prayer.

I cried out to God
fell on my face,
told the Lord Jesus
I wanted His Grace.

The woman defeated,
Jesus breaking her hold.
His powerful Spirit
now filling my soul.

Jesus Christ saved me
and made me brand new.
I'm washed in His blood
with the woman I'm through.

He's the great Shepherd
I've made Him my choice.
Whenever He calls me
I answer His voice .

Don't You Ever

Baby don't you ever,
as long as you live never.
Lift your hand
like you're the man.

Think that I'm
some ninny wimp,
who'll let you slap me
like a pimp.

Mister you're facing
one hard female,
who will never
tuck her tail.

You have surely
played the fool,
gone and made me
lose my cool.

Don't you move
cause if you do,
this gun you're facing
I'll use on you.

Lower your eyes
and don't you glare.
I'll slap you backwards
into that chair.

Shut your mouth
enoughs been said,
man don't make me
shoot you dead.

Dude I told you
to take a rest,
made me shoot you
through your chest.

Oh Dear Lord,
what have I done?
I've gone and killed
some Mama's son.

Lord I'm sorry
as I can be.
I just couldn't let him
violate me.

I watched my father
beat my mother
and terrorize
my older brother.

He was no good
deep down inside
and stripped my mother
of her pride.

Often he'd beat her
smashing her face,
fussing and cussing
and wrecking our place.

He finally passed on
but left behind,
my wounded heart
and damaged mind.

Leaving his family
with nothing at all,
but a ghetto dwelling
with grimy bare walls.

Thoughts of that man
and his evil ways,
made me vow
that cold gray day.

A man hits me
and misbehaves,
would surely find
an early grave.

I finally left home
went off to school,
a graduate with honors
and nobody's fool.

I was twenty-five,
but well educated
and landed a prize job
before I graduated.

I drove a nice ride
wore designer suits,
one confident sister
with looks to boot.

I was no china doll
to sit on a shelf,
knew martial arts
and handled myself.

Got me a handgun
obtained my permit
from that day forward
I was armed with it.

But now being faced
with this deed I've done,
I cried out to God
in the name of His Son.

I said, "Dear Lord
I don't know what to do,
with all of my heart
I call on you."

I cried out again,
as I fell to my knees.
And asked God to help me
to do something please!

That's when it happened
first time in my life.
I felt the Lord touch me
and fill me with Christ.

Yes the Lord Jesus
made the pain depart,
I felt His sweet love
as He entered my heart.

He changed my life
I was not the same,
as over and over
I whispered his name.

Suddenly I saw
the man I'd shot,
turnover on his back
and groan a lot.

How could this be?
The man was dead,
but the bullet had only
grazed his head.

He stood to his feet
and ran out the door.
I never saw or heard
from the man anymore.

The Lord yet added
to my brand-new life.
I met a sweet brother
and became his wife.

It's been five years
since I wed my man,
not one time ever
has he raised his hand.

He loves the Lord Jesus
the same as I do.
I thank God forever
for blessing us two.

He gave us children
a girl and a boy,
but Jesus is still
my pride and joy.

I know one day
His face I'll see
and thank Him forever
for saving me.

Sunshine

They called her Sunshine
I'll never forget,
that wonderful day
when we first met.

I was at the supermarket
in the ice cream isle.
I bumped her lightly
and she turned and smiled.

They called her Sunshine
and sho nuff right,
I was instantly captivated
by her pearly whites.

I'd seen smiles before,
but nothing like this.
With full luscious lips
that begged to be kissed.

I said I was sorry
I hadn't been looking,
had my mind on ice cream
and items for cooking.

Hoped I didn't hurt her
bumping her like that,
she said it was nothing
as we started to chat.

The store had a coffee shop
we sat over brew,
laughing and snacking
until well after two.

This lovely creature
where had she been.
My heart wanted nothing,
but to see her again.

She was just getting over
the last guy she'd had,
who mentally abused her
and treated her bad.

Didn't care for relationship
she said at this time,
but she'd love to go dancing
and a nice place to dine.

She gave me her number
and we left the store.
I liked what I'd found
and wanted much more.

I was in heaven
that night as I dressed,
"Thank you Lord Jesus,
you know how to bless!"

Put on a designer suit
with matching silk tie,
sprayed on fine fragrance
and knew I was fly.

I jumped in my Benz
and ran every light,
I had never been so excited
as I was that night.

She stepped from her door
in a stunning blue dress.
I heard my heart pounding
as it bumped in my chest.

I froze in my tracks
unable to move,
I had found that someone
I was not going to lose.

My head stopped spinning
I snapped back to life,
but knew in my heart
that this was my wife.

We went to a club
a small one I knew,
had an intimate setting
for a party of two.

We danced for a while
she was light on her feet.
This girl of my dreams
still smiling real sweet.

I knew how to dance
and took the lead,
put my hands on her waist
and picked up the speed.

I made her laugh
we really had fun,
I had a drink
and ordered her one.

We sat and talked
the rest of the night,
until the DJ spins
smooth Barry White.

Music for lovers
we stand to our feet.
She melts in my arms
smelling ever so sweet.

I was already sizing
her hand for a ring.
As the maestro Barry
croons and sings.

This our first date
I was acting a boy,
but my heart had sold out
and was swelling with joy.

We finally leave
and return to her place.
I kissed her forehead
she kissed my face.

"I've had a wonderful time
and made a new friend.
I can't wait," I said,
"to see you again."

Then she said,
"I had a wonderful time too
thank you so much
and glad I met you."

I left in a daze
I could barely concentrate,
my mind on Sunshine
and our wonderful date.

I called the next day
"How do you do?
Just called," I said,
"to check on you."

She said to me softly,
"You're a nice man,
but I'm not looking for ties.
I hope you understand."

"I've really been hurt.
I need time to breathe.
I can't get involved,
respect that please."

I said, "Okay,"
but really was hurt.
My heart did a dive
and drug in the dirt.

But we could have fun,
if I'd agree to keep it light.
I said I would,
we went skating that night.

Winter soon passed
and moved into spring.
I was doing serious shopping
for just the right ring.

I did keep it light
and we did just fine,
but I had a real jones
for Lady Sunshine.

I wanted to tell her
just how I felt,
how her mere presence
made my heart melt.

Seems that I kept her
always in mind.
If she had any faults
my heart was stone blind.

Finally we went
to a Sunday church meeting.
I sat with her praying
with heart wildly beating.

I said, "Dear Lord
I'll give you my life.
If you'll only give Sunshine
to me as my wife."

"I'll really work hard
to please you each day
and never hurt Sunshine
in any kind of way."

I then heard Sunshine
sobbing real low
she said, "Sweet man
I do love you so!"

"I know you're the one
the Lord has for me.
Will you please have me
as your wife to be."

I was so happy
beyond all measure.
The Lord had entrusted me
with this glorious treasure.

I said to her, "Baby,
I'll make you my wife
and vow to take care of you
the rest of my life."

We knelt at the altar
and both of us pray
and received Jesus Christ
as our savior that day.

It wasn't long after
that big day came
we exchanged our vows
in the Lord's mighty name.

I was so happy
I felt I would bust,
I vowed to let nothing
come between us.

She was my wife
and very best friend.
It seemed our honeymoon
would never have end.

A glorious new life
my Sunshine and me,
not long after
we two became three.

Little Marcella
our sweet baby girl,
the Lord Jesus sent her
to sweeten our world.

I knew that I had
a great call on my life
and was destined to preach
for the Lord Jesus Christ.

I did my first sermon
in the church we attend,
the members were clapping
and saying, "Amen"!

Each day I thank God
for these women of mine,
little Marcella
and my darling Sunshine!

A Family

I was a soldier
in a large violent gang.
I didn't have book smarts
But I knew how to bang.

Daddy left Mama
on a cold winters morn,
packed up and left us
the same day I was born.

He left us with little
and no money at all.
Never saw him again
not even one call.

Mom in depression
I took to the streets,
longing for acceptance
like a child for sweets.

I found that acceptance,
with my boys in the gang.
I became a true soldier
and learned how to bang.

I stood with my family
and gave it my best.
Tattooing my body
my back and my chest.

Addicted to thug life
I was deep into crime,
convinced if I had to
I was down to do time.

I lived for the gang fights
the small of fresh blood.
The cries of the wounded
who lie writhing in mud.

Here's where your manhood
was put to the test.
I never backed down,
but banged with the best.

Each time we would rumble
I led the attack.
Being fully persuaded
my dogs had my back.

Though giving my all
deep down in my core.
I still feared rejection
and had to do more.

The gang was my family
my really true life,
my mother, my father,
my children, my wife.

We had the girls
the gang member's toys,
but no woman on earth
took the place of my boys.

This was the Brotherhood
It replaced Mom and Dad.
No outsider understood,
the bond that we had.

All for the gang
I was willing to give.
Down for my brothers
for as long as I live.

I checked in on Mama
every few days,
gave her some money
then parted ways.

Then I met Sandra
and melted like ice.
She was so innocent
sweet pretty and nice.

Sandra was special
She was not gang life.
It wasn't very long
I wanted to make her my wife.

According to code.
She had to become part.
The thought of her joining,
brought grief to my heart.

My innocent Sandra
There'd be no such thing.
I was already shopping
for just the right ring.

I no longer loved banging
or wanted to fight.
I just wanted to be
with Sandra each night.

I now really longed,
to make her my wife.
To cease from banging
and start a new life.

I went to the leaders
and told them my mind.
Needless to say
it wasn't taken too kind.

You don't leave the gang,
you're a member for life.
Specially to make
some outsider my wife.

Take one of the sisters
get married to them,
but I wanted Sandra
my sweet little gem.

I said I was sorry,
I was tired of the life
I just wanted to leave
and make her my wife.

They told me to leave
and come back the next day,
they'd make their decision
whether I'd leave or stay.

I knew the game
and what was at stake,
you don't just leave
or simply forsake.

If I left the gang
to make Sandra my wife,
and didn't have approval
it would cost me my life.

I returned the next day
to hear their decision.
This was real life
and not television.

They hated to lose me
I was one of their best,
but if that's what I wanted
to go and be blessed.

But I had to perform
this one final job,
they had this place
they wanted me to rob.

I got my instructions
took some brothers with me,
do this last job
and I would be free.

We got to the place
I led the attack,
expecting my brothers
to cover my back.

But it was a set-up
my brothers all ran.
As police begin shouting
and giving commands.

"Drop your weapon!
Get down on your face!"
Placed in handcuffs
I'm lead from the place.

For those wanting to leave
this was a sample,
of what to expect
I was made an example.

You leave the gang
or just walk away,
there were consequences
that you had to pay.

I was now facing
five to ninety-nine.
The police had been tipped
to watch for this crime.

I had done this thing
at the leaders coercion,
but this was their payback
for my desertion.

I sat in that cell
with fear in my heart
alone and rejected
like it was at the start.

It wasn't the fact
that I feared doing time,
that wasn't the thing
that went through my mind.

It was losing my Sandra
that I faced with such dread.
Thoughts of her leaving me
was filling my head.

I became desperate
and fell to my knees,
I asked God to help me
to do something please.

I cried out to God
in the name of His Son,
if anyone could help me
I knew He was the one.

That's when it happened
in an instant that night,
Jesus came in
and pushed out the fright.

I could never describe
how I was able to see,
here was someone
who would never leave me.

The warmth and the joy
that flooded my soul,
Jesus of Nazareth
was now in control.

The Father I longed for
had now made me free.
And I knew in my heart
He would never leave me.

I fell on my face
and gave Him the praise.
I was now a real man
and knew how to behave.

It didn't make me a man
I now saw the light,
because I was a banger
and willing to fight.

I received probation
let loose on the street,
I ran to my Sandra
who was still just as sweet.

I gave her a ring
and made her my wife.
God gave us little Ronnie
to complete our life.

I now have a family
we three are one.
Thanks to my Father
and Jesus His Son.

Friday June

Mama had left us
when I was just five
and I still don't know
if she's dead or alive.

She gave me a hug
and left with some friends,
ditched my poor father
who never saw her again.

Dad moved to the country
and purchased some land.
He loved the farm life
while Mama loved bands.

She longed for the city
and bright lights again
and finally left town
with a band full of men.

That mom would return
he hoped and believed
and eight years later
my father still grieved.

She dealt my father
a miserable end,
the thoughts of his Sarah
in the arms of those men.

He finally laid down
and slept one day,
still yearning for Mama
and just slipped away.

I stood by his graveside
on a cold winter's morn,
as they lowered his vault
new hatred was born.

"Don't blame your mother,"
Father always said.
But I just couldn't help it
with Father now dead.

My mama's leaving
grieved his heart and mind.
I saw him grow old
long before time.

I alone brought joy
to his listless life,
being the spitting image
of his treacherous wife.

My father did love me
and treated me right,
but the loss of his Sarah
he just couldn't fight.

My dad's younger brother
and Megan his bride,
took me home with them
when Father had died.

This newlywed couple
took me in at thirteen.
Uncle Ray was adorable,
but Megan was mean.

I felt I was intruding
and told Uncle Ray,
who spoke to me kindly
and convinced me to stay.

I really blamed Sarah
this was her fault.
My dad would be with me
and not laid in some vault.

He had worked hard
to make her a life.
She should have been true
to her vows as a wife.

She responds to his kindness
with a knife in his back.
Probably now in the city
strung out on crack.

At the age of fifteen
I was sunning one day,
in a very small bikini
alone with Uncle Ray.

I saw him staring
and just for fun,
I struck a lewd pose
as I lay in the sun.

I then turned over
and undid my top,
but held it in place
not letting it drop.

looking behind me
I gave a small motion,
asking my Uncle
to rub me with lotion.

He sat for a moment
and didn't move at all.
"Come here Uncle Ray,"
I softly called.

He slowly arose
then fell to his knees,
the south wind blowing
a warm summer breeze.

My actions now real
it's no longer a game,
I'd been a pure virgin
both in deed and name.

He'd always been Uncle
I didn't see him as man,
but now I lay burning
for the touch of his hands.

I felt his hands tremble
and their warm impact,
as he poured on lotion
and rubbed my back.

we both crossed the line
our flesh on fire,
we yield to temptation
and fulfill our desire.

For the next three years
we lived a double life,
our well kept secret
from the town and his wife.

We knew it was incest
sinful and wrong,
but Uncle was handsome
considerate and strong.

He bought me nice things
and he'd take me away,
to strange new places
where we'd openly play.

One day at home
my Uncle came in
and proceeded to tell me
he was through with our sin.

I fell on his neck
and told him no way.
God would forgive us
if we would just pray.

Preachers did stuff
and got caught all the time.
We didn't have to stop
he could still be mine.

He disengaged my arms
and said he was through.
No words I could say
and nothing I could do.

I was devastated
and hurt to my heart.
I had thought that nothing
would pull us apart.

He'd told me he loved me
even more than his wife.
That I was that special
someone in his life.

Now he was dumping me
like Sarah did Dad.
I was raging inside
and burning hot mad.

You're supposed to commit
to people you love.
you don't throw them away
like a worn-out glove.

He'd be sorry for this
I would make him pay.
I wasn't my dad
to walk quietly away.

I went to the police
and proceeded to tell,
of our three-year tryst
in lurid detail.

I gave them receipts
from our rendezvous,
two day rentals
of cottages for two.

I showed them pictures
of lover's embraces,
romantic smiles
in each others faces.

Sentimental cards
with romantic lines
and thanks from Uncle
for our intimate times.

My evidence was solid
justice quickly dispensed,
that I had enticed him
was his only defense.

Uncle took a plea
and they gave him five years.
He stood there sobbing
and drowning in tears.

But I felt nothing
he deserved what he got,
he should've been locked up
in a cell to rot.

If I could find mother
I'd punish her too.
She'd regret she had me
when I was through.

At age eighteen
I was out on the streets
and worked a café
to make ends meet.

There I met Damon
who was raised in L.A.
and was visiting his aunt
for a very short stay.

Damon and I
had a whirlwind romance
when his time came to leave
I grabbed my chance.

I left town with Damon
to start a new life,
hoping that soon
he'd make me his wife.

I'd stand by him
through thick and thin,
the way real women
stand by their men.

We drove to Los Angeles
and got a hotel suite.
Damon soon left me
to get something to eat.

He left very agitated,
but returned with a smile.
This happened several times
in a very short while.

I became suspicious
and searched our room.
I found Damon's eyedropper
his needle and spoon.

This man is a drug addict
I now clearly see,
the impact of it all
was overwhelming for me.

I confronted Damon
the moment he came back,
who fell to his knees
and showed me his tracks.

He was hooked on heroin
for the last three years
and just couldn't stop
he told me with tears.

If I'd stand by him
he was sure he could kick,
I remained there with him
and watched him grow sick.

The worse smell on earth
had filled our room,
like a rotting corpse
cast out of its tomb.

His withdrawal symptoms
like nothing I'd seen,
I fell to my knees
asking God to intervene.

I wouldn't leave Damon
though I'm not his wife,
I can't turn on my man
at this low point in his life.

I made God a promise
if He brought him through
I said, "Dear God
I'll live for you!"

And God did move
and Damon did kick,
from that day forward
he was no longer sick.

I remembered the promise
I made God that day
and found a small church
in South Central L.A.

I knelt at the altar
and called on Jesus Christ.
He instantly answered
and entered my life.

Damon saw the change
that Jesus made in me
and came to church too
and has been made free.

For five years now
I've been Damon's wife
we have three children
and joy in our life.

There's none like Jesus
who has made us his own
who will never forsake
or leave us alone.

I know He'll never
just walk off and leave.
He's lived inside me
since the day I believed.

I've forgiven poor Sarah
and Uncle Ray too.
I know my Lord loves me
and he's mad about you.

Hornet's Nest

I was a soldier
in the civil war
President Lincoln
had gone too far.

At least that's what they said
way down south
and had fired on Ft. Sumter
after running their mouth.

The National Union
they intended to end,
but the north came forth
calling up her men.

I had enlisted
as a raw volunteer.
Doing my duty
laying aside my career.

Not to oppose slavery
or opposed to owning men,
but simply to bring the south
into the union again.

I had drilled and drilled
and drilled some more.
Marching and marching
til my legs were sore.

Finally they declared
I was fit to serve,
I left boot camp
with a lot of hot nerve.

It was then declared
that I had the stomach,
to now be a part
of the Army of the Potomac.

We felt it would be quick
the south would yield.
Til we met those rebels
on the battle field.

Our first encounter
at the Battle of Bull Run.
There in terror
we dropped our guns.

Turned ourselves about
and fled in fright.
Limped back to Washington
in defeat that night.

We'd learned our lesson
this war was real.
I prayed to God
that I wouldn't get killed.

At the Sunken Road
and the Hornet's Nest too,
many fierce battles
God took me through.

First time I'd ever
seen grown men cry.
Building God an altar
not wanting to die.

The Battle of Chickamauga
and Fredericksburg as well.
We battled in defeat
and came through hell.

We were surrounded
by the wounded and dead,
as Bullets and cannon balls
whizzed over our heads.

But there at Gettysburg
Joshua Chamberlain plants feet,
won the Battle of Little Round Top
beginning the South's defeat.

There in the Deep South
I saw horrible sights.
Enough to convince me
that slavery wasn't right.

No man has the right
to keep another in chains.
Slaves had endured
much misery and pain.

The land of the free
and the home of the brave,
these Seemed hollow words
to those made slaves.

To this evil institution
and darkest of sin.
Men felt they were entitled
by the color of their skin.

To be owned by another
and told what to do,
that set limitations
and humiliated you.

We held this people's
fate in our hands.
We must free them now
and cleanse our land.

They fled out to us
thousands at a time,
what has been done to them
still boggles my mind.

William Tecumseh Sherman
setting men free,
as he tore through Atlanta
on his march to the sea.

His scorched earth policy
gave the South a fright,
as the armies of the Potomac
burned everything in sight.

The army of Northern Virginia
under Robert E. Lee,
their backs to the wall now
had to turn and flee.

The two armies met
at Bull Run once more.
This time it was different
the North settled the score.

But in the midst of battle
I saw the light,
I really found Jesus
and refused to fight.

I followed large battles
for the rest of the war
and saved men's lives
in the Medical Corps.

Finally at Appomattox
General Lee gives in,
Grant saved the Union
we were one again.

It hadn't been in vain,
Union men that fell.
And the scourge of slavery
had ended as well.

With charity toward all
and malice toward none,
President Lincoln asks all men
to lay down their guns.

It all came to an end
in eighteen sixty-five,
I was thankful to God
I was still alive.

Yes I was alive,
but thankful the most,
He saved me and filled me
with the Holy Ghost.

I preached Christ Jesus
to all that would hear,
preaching His truth
for the rest of my years.

President Lincoln and Grant
Generals Longstreet and Lee,
but Jesus still reigned
so mightily in me.

Nadine

Hi their friend,
my name is Nadine.
A real street sister
I'm hardened and mean.

Sometimes I remember
and it still makes me sad.
How I turned out for Kevin,
The first pimp that I had.

Kevin was young then,
but known on the streets.
His uncles were gangsters,
hustlers and cheats.

We met at a block party,
one late summer night.
Kevin worked out
and his muscles were tight.

He had that confidence,
a man that takes charge.
The moment I met him,
I dumped my friend marge.

My eyes couldn't drink up,
enough of this man.
I melted like butter,
at the touch of his hand.

Kevin knew hustle,
but I was barely eighteen.
When it came to street life,
he knew I was green.

I hung out with Kevin
and met some of his friends.
He then took me home,
in his brand new Benz.

I was ready to make out,
Kevin said he would call.
He didn't try to kiss me,
or touch me at all.

I was so disappointed,
my head spinning round.
But walked to my door,
with my feet off the ground.

Later that week,
he picked me up in his Benz.
And took me to party,
with his uncles and friends.

This was a rough crowd,
But I didn't fear harm.
I felt so protected,
as I danced in his arms.

Kevin treated me sweet,
like I was his bride.
He gave me his attention,
never leaving my side.

He made me feel special
and melted my heart.
I was head over heels,
right from the start.

Kevin soon asked me,
to live at his place.
And I picked up my things,
with all due haste.

We lived with his uncles,
in a two story pad.
Never a dull moment
and fun to be had.

But we always had time,
for intimate talks.
And did things together.
like late evening walks

But Kevin became distant,
with drastic mood swings.
He still kept me with him,
but was silent about things.

Finally he told me,
he was in a tight fix.
If he didn't get cash,
he'd have to leave quick.

I couldn't go with him,
I'd have to go home.
And I went for the bait,
like a dog for a bone.

I maybe could help him,
If I did care enough.
He was facing real danger
and things would get rough.

He said he could fix it,
If he had enough cash.
The mob was after him
and he'd have to move fast.

He knew of this guy,
who made adult films.
If I really did care,
I'd do this for him.

He'd contact the guy,
I'd star in some sets.
And make enough cash,
to pay off his debts.

I looked at this man,
stunned to the core.
Did he really expect *me*,
to perform like a whore?

How could he think,
I would do such a thing?
I felt my face flush
and heard my ears ring.

How could he ask this?
If he cared for me?
I don't even know him,
I now clearly see.

Kevin responded,
to the look on my face.
By packing his things,
to leave the place.

He picked up his bags,
to walk out the door.
It was then I collapsed
and fell to the floor.

I cried to him, "Baby,
I'll do what you say!"
I just couldn't handle,
him walking away.

He dropped both his bags
and began kissing my face.
While holding me close,
in a tender embrace.

Later that week,
we went to the set.
And I was shocked to see,
some of his friends I'd met.

One had a camera
and he starts giving tips.
On how to play out,
some so called script.

I then said to Kevin
"This can't go down.
Me turning tricks,
on film with these clowns."

He said to me patiently,
"Baby I do understand,
just thought you were down,
with helping your man.

If we hired regular actors,
we'd have to pay cash.
My homies are here,
to help me build stash.

If it's asking too much,
I'll leave town tonight.
Bounce to the airport
and catch the next flight."

His game was so smooth,
that I bought it again.
Held out for a while,
but finally caved in.

I went through the motions,
with several of his friends.
Worst time in my life,
was spent with those men.

When it finally was over,
I felt so abused.
Degraded and ashamed
and totally misused.

He'd made me feel special,
Kevin melting my heart.
But it was nothing but game
from the very start.

It was all a sham,
his grand master plan.
To turn this girl out,
to meet his demands.

He didn't rush things,
the man took his time.
And carefully groomed,
his raw little find.

It was never a porn film.
I found out later,
he used this deception,
to become my dictator.

He had planned all along,
to make me his whore.
And had to make sure,
I didn't walk out the door.

He'd send copies,
to my family and friends.
Showing me romping,
with all of those men.

I said to Kevin,
"Why do this to me?
The fact that I love you,
I know you can see."

Kevin acted coldly,
like I was nothing to him.
And kept talking crazy,
about using that film.

"I knew you'd trick,
right from the start.
Just had to show you,
it was down in your heart.

I don't fall in love,
like some trick lame.
I'm a true player baby,
getting paid is my game.

You'll do what I say
and get down on the streets.
Or I'll fix your mouth,
where you can't even eat.

If I tell you to leap,
you'd better ask how high.
And you've got plenty,
of what tricks want to buy.

I've got just the place,
to put out on the stem.
To parade your wares,
in front of them."

And for fourteen years,
a long list of men.
Would use my body,
for degenerate sin.

I had many pimps,
throughout those years.
But none like Kevin,
brought me to tears.

I really did love him,
with all that I had.
His reward was to play me
and hurt me real bad.

I heard years later,
Kevin burned to death.
His lab caught fire,
while cooking meth.

But I met this preacher,
on the stroll one day.
Who asked me politely,
about letting him pray.

He said Jesus died,
to set us all free.
And had special love,
for hurting people like me.

I did bow my head,
and allowed him to pray.
He gave me a smile,
and then walked away.

Later that night,
as I lay in my bed.
The words of the preacher,
were alive in my head.

I thought about Kevin
and how I was used.
The love I had offered,
he totally refused.

Then thought about Jesus,
who paid such a cost.
coming down from heaven,
To die for the lost.

Seeing this great love,
The Lord had for me.
I knew from the old life,
I could finally be free.

Down on the stroll,
I watched every day.
For that God sent preacher,
to return my way.

Finally I saw him,
With his Bible in hand.
I ran across the street
and confronted the man.

I stood there a prostitute,
with slits up my thighs.
But I only saw love,
pour from his eyes.

I said I was ready,
for change in my life.
And the man introduced me,
to the Lord Jesus Christ.

He took me to church,
where I was baptized.
Bringing joy to my heart
and tears to his eyes.

Its five years' now
and I married that man.
Who came to the stroll,
with his Bible in hand.

And Jesus is still,
our ultimate joy.
And has given us children,
two girls and a boy.

From all of my filth,
Jesus washed me clean.
And made Him a lady,
out of sister Nadine.

Jesse Don't Play

The dude was finished
for him no hope,
nobody burns Jessie
with counterfeit dope.

I go to my pad
and grab my heat.
fussing and cussing
and stomping my feet.

I break from my door
like a bird from his cage,
squeal from my driveway
roaring with rage.

I turn the corner
and wheel down the street,
planning to waste him
the moment we meet.

Entering the freeway
I really get riled,
my rage was growing with
each passing mile.

I'll blow that turkey
right out of his shoes,
his name will be broadcast
on six o'clock news.

Nobody rips me
and then gets away.
I'll let it be known
that Jessie don't play.

I went to the corner
where the dude got down,
hand on my piece
and looking around.

I couldn't find a trace,
but I was not going to quit.
Fussing and cussing
and throwing a fit.

The chump had faded
and left the streets.
My ears were roaring
as my heart wildly beats.

What was he thinking?
That I would just chill?
That I wouldn't come armed
with an intent to kill?

My head now pounding
from clinching my jaws,
not even conscious
of cruising city laws.

My eyes are slits
and totally bloodshot,
I'd leave this monkey
in the bushes to rot.

But something tells me
to leave the place,
as around and around
the block I pace.

But there was no way
I'd let this go down,
you back down once
and word gets around.

Let this dude go?
There was no way,
now everyone will know
that Jessie don't play.

From behind a building
I see a quick flash.
The trick I was looking for
made a mad dash.

I made my run too
and began closing in,
he'd better ask God
to forgive his sins.

I pulled out my piece
and fired off a round,
and a child flew backward
and fell to the ground.

I instantly realized
what I'd now done.
Gone and put a bullet
in some mama's small son.

I stopped in my tracks
and fell to my knees,
as officers pull up
and tell me to freeze.

"Don't let him die God!"
I desperately pray.
I hadn't intended
things going this way.

"Don't let him die God!"
I cried out again
and asking the Lord
to forgive me this sin.

Locked in the squad car
thoughts flooding my head,
what would I do
if the child is now dead.

They'd make me a home
on the state's death row.
How was he doing?
I just had to know.

Carried to city,
I'm printed and booked.
God only knows
how horrible I looked.

All my big talk
of gunning the dude down,
instead a small child
had taken the round.

My deranged temper
which turned on a dime,
has got me a death sentence
or a long stretch of time.

I lay on my bunk
praying all night,
asking God to help me
and to make things right.

I promised the Lord
if He'd let the child live,
I'd repent of my sins
and my life to Him give.

The very next morning
I was able to make bail
and good news awaited
as I walked out of jail.

When my gun fired
Mama hearing the sound,
through her arm backward
and knocked the child down.

The blow to the child
lifted him off his feet,
knocking him unconscious
as his head hit the street.

God had been listening
as I prayed on that bed,
and I gave Him my life
just as I said.

I received probation
for my violent act
and I left the dope game
and never looked back.

I've kept every promise
I made Jesus that day.
Yes God is my record
that Jessie don't play.

Emerald

I had been an executive
with a promising career.
Until putting a "c note,"
in a strippers brazier.

Called herself Emerald
and none of her fake,
performing on stage
with a "Bo Strictor" snake.

"Charlie" would crawl up
and wrap around her leg,
then sway to the music
while seeming to beg.

She'd cup her hands
in back of his head,
then kiss ole Charlie
who'd appear to drop dead.

Ever so slowly,
Charlie seemed to revive.
As Emerald peeped over him
with alluring green eyes.

The woman bewitched me
it was more than just fun,
I was trembling all over
when her act was done.

Her provocative routine
made my knees shake.
I wanted to have her,
but minus the snake.

I gave her more money
and a note I'd scrawled,
containing my phone number
and asked her to call.

She didn't waste time,
but called the next day,
but I found myself lost
for right words to say.

I need not have worried
she saw the light,
and ask me to come back
to the club that night.

I returned to a smile
which didn't seem fake,
that night I went home
with her and the snake.

She said to me sweetly,
"Do you know who I am?
You just entered boot camp
and I'm Uncle Sam."

"Pick up your back pack
tie your boots on tight,
I'll be giving the orders
the rest of this night."

Emerald took charge
and did make believe.
I was totally enslaved
by the time that I leave.

The days that followed
found me totally debased,
paying all the bills
and rent at her place.

I left momma's home
and finally moved in,
Emerald now pulling me
deeper into sin.

She asked me to help her
one night in late June,
it was then she produced
her needle and spoon.

She begged for assistance
to find a good vein,
I said "you're crazy,
and totally insane!"

She pleaded and begged
and began to pout,
till all my resistance
was totally wiped out.

She often did heroin
and tempted me sore,
saying I would fly
if I too would score.

We could make love
on a whole new plane,
holding my arms
while caressing my veins.

One night I laid back
as she tied off my arm,
finally brought under
by her persuasive charms.

A rush of pure ecstasy
like nothing I'd dreamed,
Queen Heroin became
my Lord Supreme.

No way to describe
that rush in detail,
but Emerald had put me
on a pathway to hell.

She began to shoot heroin
with a low dose of speed,
till finally one day
I found her o'deed.

From that time on
it was a swift descent,
I was grieved at her death,
but wouldn't repent.

My grieving didn't stop me
from getting the shakes,
having ever shot heroin
was a massive mistake.

Broke and addicted
and stripped of my pride.
I finally sold Charlie
and my broken-down ride.

Years drifted by
and I couldn't break free.
The rehabs and programs
doing nothing for me.

I'd leave the rehabs
after trying to kick smack,
with that terrible monkey
still riding my back.

Strung out on heroin
for too many years,
I'd broke momma's heart
and reduced her to tears.

How had this happened
to her once proud son,
how had I become
a junkie and con.

Mama would look at me
with despair and alarm,
praying I didn't die
with a spike in my arm.

The life of a junkie
a pure and living hell.
We all should be gathered
and carried to jail.

Not even read rights,
but snatched off the streets
and cast into prison
with chains on our feet.

It would be more merciful
if they did that to me,
than live as a junkie
who can never be free.

The battle never ended
I was faced each day,
with a habit grown bigger
and harder to pay.

That woman called Heroin
had now become God,
I'd worship her daily
if she'd just let me "nod."

My whole life was spent
chasing that whore,
she knew I'd do anything
to cop my next score.

I'd steal from my mother
and grandmother too.
Pawn all their goods
and sell their last shoe.

But one day reality
flooded in on me,
as there in a window
my reflection I see.

I couldn't believe it
this couldn't be true
I said to myself,
"That can't be you!"

My looks are all gone
and "smack" is to blame,
the face staring at me
made me ashamed.

"Lord what happened?"
I heard myself cry
"What happened Lord?
Please tell me why"

"The price of sin,"
I heard the Lord say
"The wages are death
and you surely will pay."

The years of filth
my shame and sin,
on waves of sorrow
came crashing right in.

I fell on my face
and said real low,
"I'm sorry Lord Jesus
I just didn't know."

A voice then said,
"If you want a new start,
call upon Jesus
with all of your heart."

It was a sweet brother
I had come to know,
thank God for Preachers
who visit skid row.

I called upon Jesus
and felt such release,
my shame is replaced
with deep settled peace.

I looked at my arms
not even a track.
And no more monkey
is riding my back.

Jesus has saved me
and cleansed me within
and gave me His Spirit
in place of my sins.

I'm no more a junkie
my head is now clear,
I now preach the gospel
to all who will hear.

Talk of new creatures
I'm new as can be,
cause only in Jesus
are junkies made free.

On The Run

My heart was pounding
as there I lay,
hiding in the bushes
most of the day.

Nobody would ever
tell me again,
what I could do
where and when.

My name is Lester
from sweet county line.
I knew I could never
do more time.

I did a bit
five years I spent,
locked behind bars
without one cent.

At last I'm freed
had made parole,
got me a job
and did as told.

I did my job,
came to work each day.
Put in eight hours
and looked for pay.

My pay is short
and I don't know why,
then see the manager
passing by.

I asked him why
my pay was short.
He gave to me
a curt retort.

This dissing me
would not stand,
I would not be treated
less than a man.

I wanted my money
I told him there.
He smarts again
and I grab a chair.

Suddenly I'm seeing
nothing but red
and bring a blow
upside his head.

I whipped him there,
all over the place.
Til blood was flowing
from his face.

Now I'm out here,
on the run.
Hiding in the bushes
for what I've done.

I see her laying
on her bed.
Brown and sassy
and hair real red.

I had been watching
most of the day.
She was alone
and easy prey.

I began to crawl
toward her place.
I'm fascinated
by her face.

She was at ease
and didn't know,
I was watching her
from the shrubs below.

I crawled on my belly
nice and smooth,
not making a sound
as I moved.

I'd find a spot
and bust right in.
Catch her off guard
as I'm coming in.

I hated to disturb her
on her bed,
but the thought of bars
fills me with dread.

Five years was enough
for any man.
I was not going back
to any State's can.

They treat you like cattle
not men at all,
once they have you
behind those walls.

Never again
will I live like that,
like some insect
or some lab rat.

I needed a way
to make a break,
I'd take her car
for freedoms sake.

I'll take her with me
part of the way,
I can't remain here
til break of day.

I find a window
and easy as juice,
I take my knife
and pry it loose.

I need a car
and I won't repent,
as quickly through
the window I went.

But heard the Lord,
speak to me that night,
"What you're doing Lester
Just isn't right."

"Go back the way
you just came in.
I'll make you whole
and cleanse your sin."

Out the window
I went back through.
And closed it back
like I was told to do.

I looked for the Preacher
I knew would be there.
He'd sent them before,
His gospel to share.

But I wouldn't listen
or change my way,
but that night was different
as I kneeled to pray

I told Lord Jesus
I was ready to give in,
tired of running
and living in sin.

He did send a Preacher
to me that night,
who showed me how
to get my heart right.

I turned myself in
they added to me
a year in prison,
a month later I'm free.

I have a new job
and there treating me right.
And I'm saved by Jesus
like He promised me that night.

That red headed woman
is saved too you see,
and that's not all
but married to me.

Just as it is written
and the Lord has spoken,
a three-fold cord
is not quickly broken.

We have a dear son
he's one year old.
When God made him,
He broke the mold.

I tell everybody
that will listen to me,
that Christ is the answer
the only way to be free.

Dedication

This book is dedicated to the Glory of God
and our Lord and Savior Jesus Christ.

Connect With the Author

E-mail: LoosedbyJesus@gmail.com
Facebook: https://www.facebook.com/Loosed-326294607787305/
Church: https://www.facebook.com/TheLordsHouseHouston/
Outreach Ministry: www.thelordshouseoutreach.com

Join us in person:

The Lord's House
2501 McGowen St
Houston, Texas 77004

Tuesday: 7:00 pm – 10:00 pm Thursday: 7:00 pm – 10:00pm
Sunday School: 10:00am to 12:00 noon Worship: 12 noon -3:00pm

Made in the USA
Middletown, DE
04 December 2022

15876798R00044